this
Prayer Journal

BELONGS TO:

....

DATE RECEIVED:

....

Psalms 139 v 13-14

"For you formed
my inward parts;
you knitted me together
in my mother's womb.

I praise you, for I am fearfully and
wonderfully made.

Wonderful are your works;
my soul knows it
very well."

Today's Date

Daily Verse

Thoughts / Reflections

I am thankful for

Prayer Requests

Today's Date

Daily Verse

Thoughts / Reflections

I am thankful for

Prayer Requests

Today's Date

Daily Verse

Thoughts / Reflections

I am thankful for

Prayer Requests

Today's Date

Daily Verse

Thoughts / Reflections

I am thankful for

Prayer Requests

Today's Date

Daily Verse

Thoughts / Reflections

I am thankful for

Prayer Requests

Today's Date

Daily Verse

Thoughts / Reflections

I am thankful for

Prayer Requests

Today's Date

Daily Verse

Thoughts / Reflections

I am thankful for

Prayer Requests

Today's Date

Daily Verse

Thoughts / Reflections

I am thankful for

Prayer Requests

Today's Date

Daily Verse

Thoughts / Reflections

I am thankful for

Prayer Requests

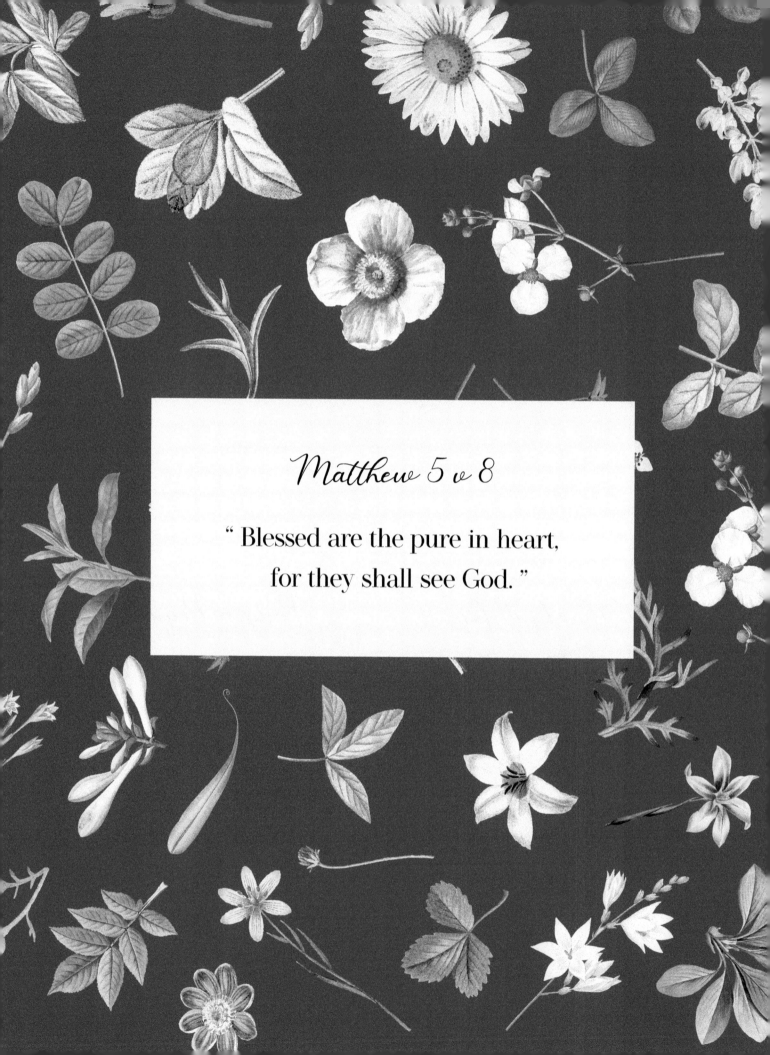

Matthew 5 v 8

" Blessed are the pure in heart, for they shall see God. "

Today's Date

Daily Verse

Thoughts / Reflections

I am thankful for

Prayer Requests

Today's Date

Daily Verse

Thoughts / Reflections

I am thankful for

Prayer Requests

Today's Date

Daily Verse

Thoughts / Reflections

I am thankful for

Prayer Requests

Today's Date

Daily Verse

Thoughts / Reflections

I am thankful for

Prayer Requests

Today's Date

Daily Verse

Thoughts / Reflections

I am thankful for

Prayer Requests

Today's Date

Daily Verse

Thoughts / Reflections

I am thankful for

Prayer Requests

Today's Date

Daily Verse

Thoughts / Reflections

I am thankful for

Prayer Requests

Today's Date

Daily Verse

Thoughts / Reflections

I am thankful for

Prayer Requests

Today's Date

Daily Verse

Thoughts / Reflections

I am thankful for

Prayer Requests

Zephaniah 3 v 17

"The Lord your God
is in your midst,
a mighty one
who will save;
he will rejoice over
you with gladness;
he will quiet you
by his love;
he will exult over you
with loud singing."

Today's Date

Daily Verse

Thoughts / Reflections

I am thankful for

Prayer Requests

Today's Date

Daily Verse

Thoughts / Reflections

I am thankful for

Prayer Requests

Today's Date

Daily Verse

Thoughts / Reflections

I am thankful for

Prayer Requests

Today's Date

Daily Verse

Thoughts / Reflections

I am thankful for

Prayer Requests

Today's Date

Daily Verse

Thoughts / Reflections

I am thankful for

Prayer Requests

Today's Date

Daily Verse

Thoughts / Reflections

I am thankful for

Prayer Requests

Today's Date

Daily Verse

Thoughts / Reflections

I am thankful for

Prayer Requests

Today's Date

Daily Verse

Thoughts / Reflections

I am thankful for

Prayer Requests

Today's Date

Daily Verse

Thoughts / Reflections

I am thankful for

Prayer Requests

Psalms 136 v 26

" Give thanks
to the God of heaven,
for his steadfast love
endures forever."

Today's Date

Daily Verse

Thoughts / Reflections

I am thankful for

Prayer Requests

Today's Date

Daily Verse

Thoughts / Reflections

I am thankful for

Prayer Requests

Today's Date

Daily Verse

Thoughts / Reflections

I am thankful for

Prayer Requests

Today's Date

Daily Verse

Thoughts / Reflections

I am thankful for

Prayer Requests

Today's Date

Daily Verse

Thoughts / Reflections

I am thankful for

Prayer Requests

Today's Date

Daily Verse

Thoughts / Reflections

I am thankful for

Prayer Requests

Today's Date

Daily Verse

Thoughts / Reflections

I am thankful for

Prayer Requests

Today's Date

Daily Verse

Thoughts / Reflections

I am thankful for

Prayer Requests

Today's Date

Daily Verse

Thoughts / Reflections

I am thankful for

Prayer Requests

1 John 4 v 16

"So we have come to know
and to believe the love
that God has for us.

God is love, and whoever abides
in love abides in God,
and God abides in him."

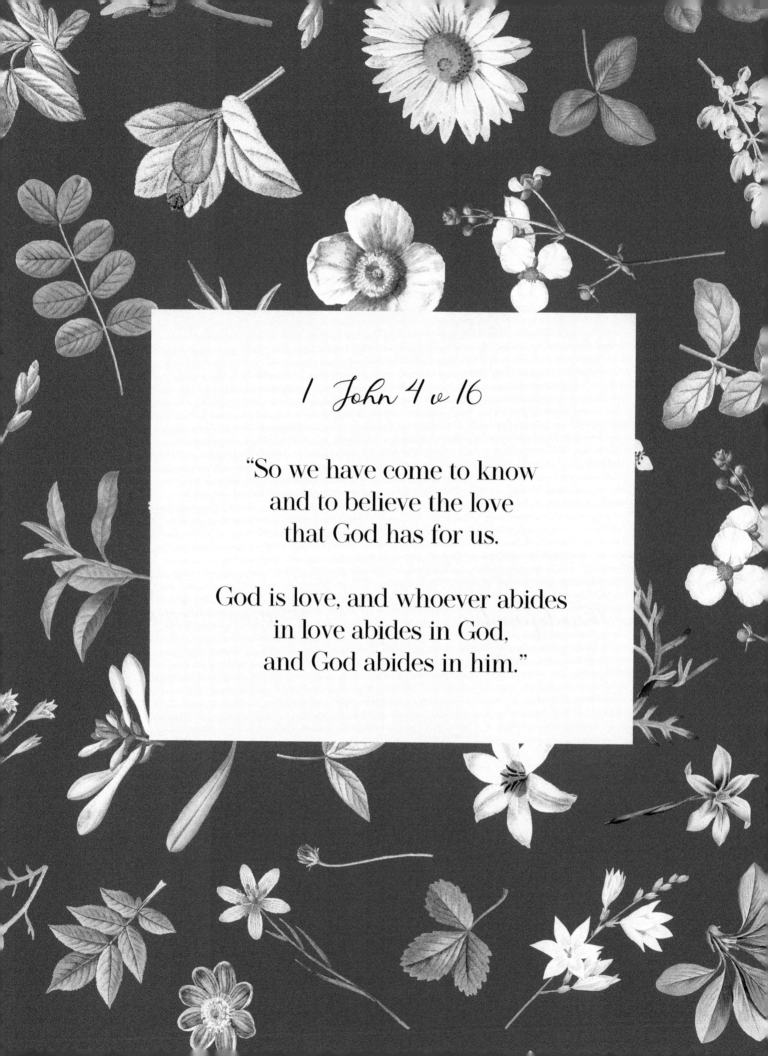

Today's Date

Daily Verse

Thoughts / Reflections

I am thankful for

Prayer Requests

Today's Date

Daily Verse

Thoughts / Reflections

I am thankful for

Prayer Requests

Today's Date

Daily Verse

Thoughts / Reflections

I am thankful for

Prayer Requests

Today's Date

Daily Verse

Thoughts / Reflections

I am thankful for

Prayer Requests

Today's Date

Daily Verse

Thoughts / Reflections

I am thankful for

Prayer Requests

Today's Date	
Daily Verse	Thoughts / Reflections
I am thankful for	Prayer Requests

Today's Date

Daily Verse

Thoughts / Reflections

I am thankful for

Prayer Requests

Today's Date

Daily Verse

Thoughts / Reflections

I am thankful for

Prayer Requests

Today's Date

Daily Verse

Thoughts / Reflections

I am thankful for

Prayer Requests

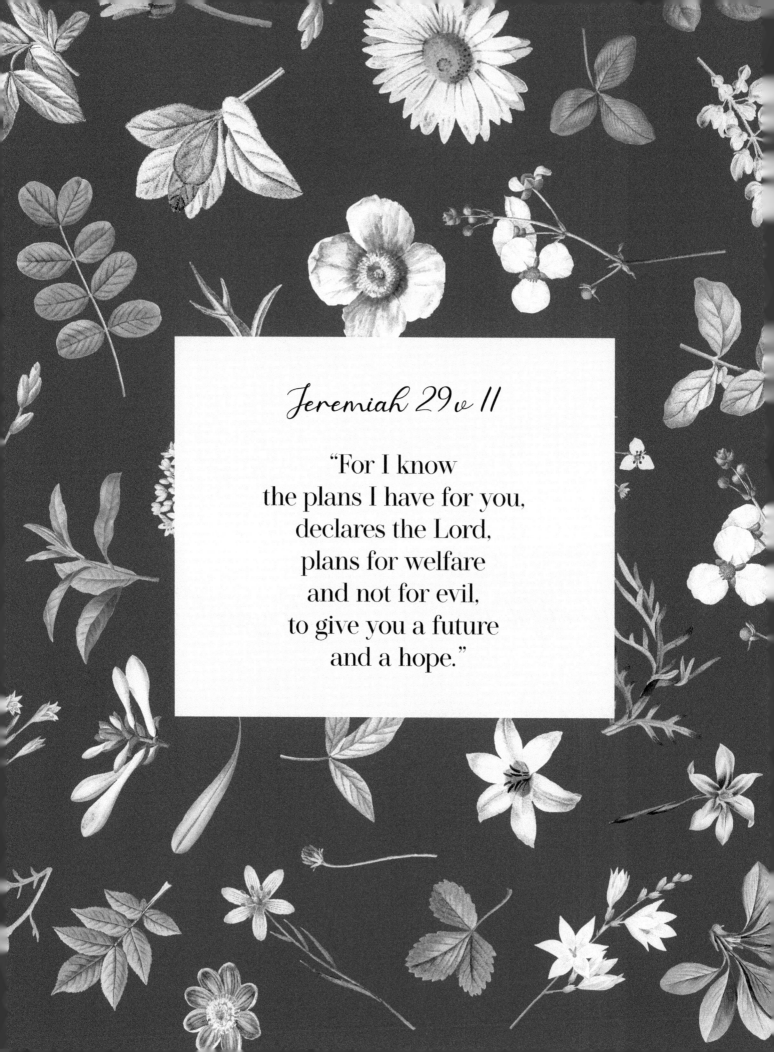

Today's Date

Daily Verse

Thoughts / Reflections

I am thankful for

Prayer Requests

Today's Date

Daily Verse

Thoughts / Reflections

I am thankful for

Prayer Requests

Today's Date

Daily Verse

Thoughts / Reflections

I am thankful for

Prayer Requests

Today's Date

Daily Verse

Thoughts / Reflections

I am thankful for

Prayer Requests

Today's Date

Daily Verse

Thoughts / Reflections

I am thankful for

Prayer Requests

Today's Date

Daily Verse

Thoughts / Reflections

I am thankful for

Prayer Requests

Today's Date	
Daily Verse	**Thoughts / Reflections**
I am thankful for	**Prayer Requests**

Today's Date

Daily Verse

Thoughts / Reflections

I am thankful for

Prayer Requests

Today's Date

Daily Verse

Thoughts / Reflections

I am thankful for

Prayer Requests

Proverbs 3 v 5-6

" Trust in the Lord
with all your heart,
and do not lean
on your own understanding.

In all your ways
acknowledge him,
and he will make
straight your paths."

Today's Date

Daily Verse

Thoughts / Reflections

I am thankful for

Prayer Requests

Today's Date

Daily Verse

Thoughts / Reflections

I am thankful for

Prayer Requests

Today's Date

Daily Verse

Thoughts / Reflections

I am thankful for

Prayer Requests

Today's Date

Daily Verse

Thoughts / Reflections

I am thankful for

Prayer Requests

Today's Date

Daily Verse

Thoughts / Reflections

I am thankful for

Prayer Requests

Today's Date

Daily Verse

Thoughts / Reflections

I am thankful for

Prayer Requests

Today's Date

Daily Verse

Thoughts / Reflections

I am thankful for

Prayer Requests

Today's Date

Daily Verse

Thoughts / Reflections

I am thankful for

Prayer Requests

Today's Date

Daily Verse

Thoughts / Reflections

I am thankful for

Prayer Requests

1 John 5 v 14-16

" This is the confidence that we have toward him, that if we ask anything according to his will he hears us.

And if we know that he hears us in whatever we ask, we know that we have the requests that we have asked of him."

Today's Date

Daily Verse

Thoughts / Reflections

I am thankful for

Prayer Requests

Today's Date

Daily Verse

Thoughts / Reflections

I am thankful for

Prayer Requests

Today's Date

Daily Verse

Thoughts / Reflections

I am thankful for

Prayer Requests

Today's Date	
Daily Verse	Thoughts / Reflections
I am thankful for	Prayer Requests

Today's Date

Daily Verse

Thoughts / Reflections

I am thankful for

Prayer Requests

Today's Date

Daily Verse

Thoughts / Reflections

I am thankful for

Prayer Requests

Today's Date

Daily Verse

Thoughts / Reflections

I am thankful for

Prayer Requests

Today's Date

Daily Verse

Thoughts / Reflections

I am thankful for

Prayer Requests

Today's Date

Daily Verse

Thoughts / Reflections

I am thankful for

Prayer Requests

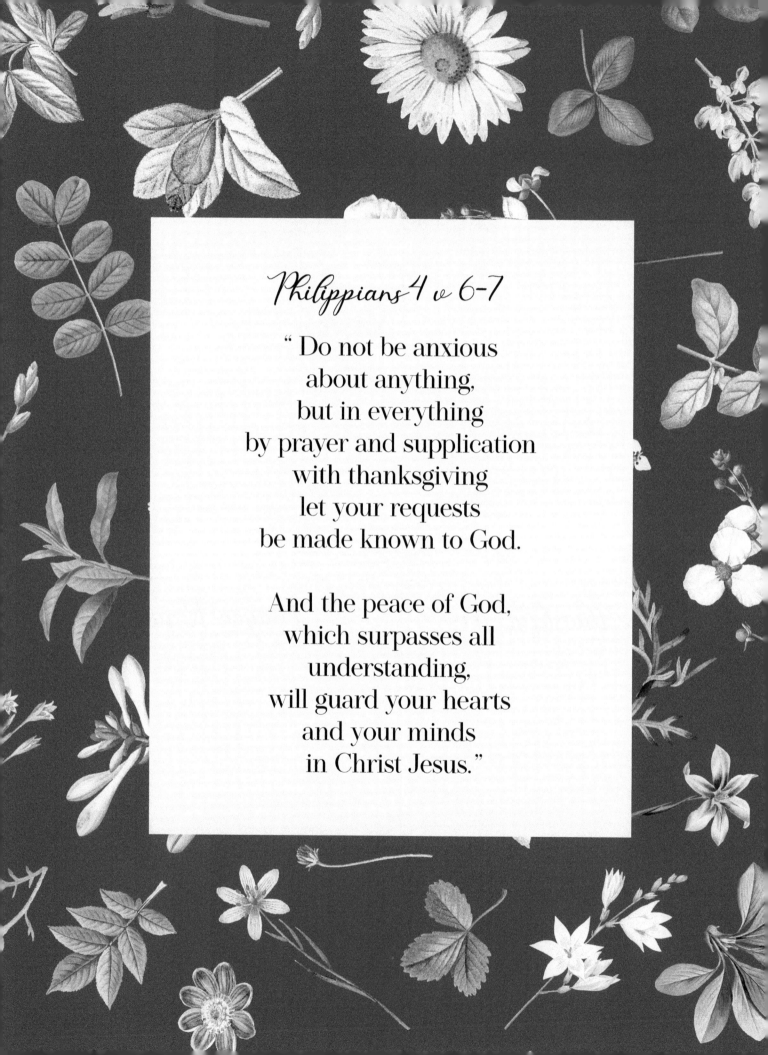

Today's Date

Daily Verse

Thoughts / Reflections

I am thankful for

Prayer Requests

Today's Date

Daily Verse

Thoughts / Reflections

I am thankful for

Prayer Requests

Today's Date

Daily Verse

Thoughts / Reflections

I am thankful for

Prayer Requests

Today's Date

Daily Verse

Thoughts / Reflections

I am thankful for

Prayer Requests

Today's Date

Daily Verse

Thoughts / Reflections

I am thankful for

Prayer Requests

Today's Date

Daily Verse

Thoughts / Reflections

I am thankful for

Prayer Requests

Today's Date

Daily Verse

Thoughts / Reflections

I am thankful for

Prayer Requests

Today's Date

Daily Verse

Thoughts / Reflections

I am thankful for

Prayer Requests

Today's Date

Daily Verse

Thoughts / Reflections

I am thankful for

Prayer Requests

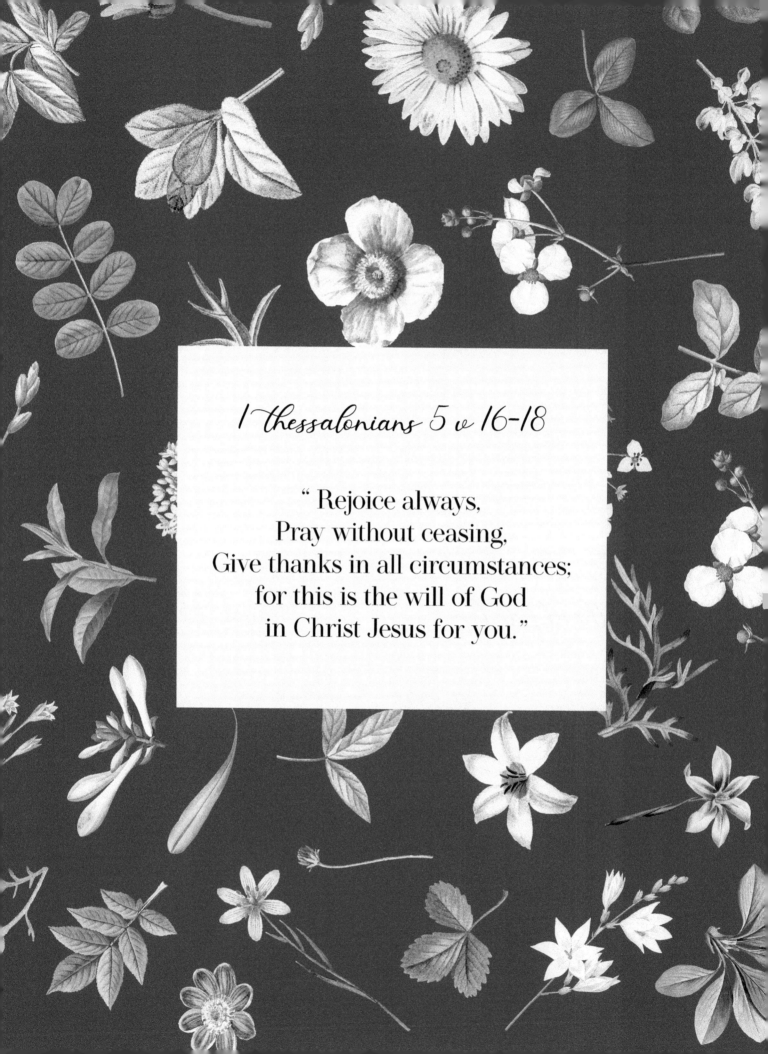

1 Thessalonians 5 v 16-18

" Rejoice always,
Pray without ceasing,
Give thanks in all circumstances;
for this is the will of God
in Christ Jesus for you."

Today's Date

Daily Verse

Thoughts / Reflections

I am thankful for

Prayer Requests

Today's Date

Daily Verse

Thoughts / Reflections

I am thankful for

Prayer Requests

Today's Date

Daily Verse

Thoughts / Reflections

I am thankful for

Prayer Requests

Today's Date

Daily Verse

Thoughts / Reflections

I am thankful for

Prayer Requests

Today's Date

Daily Verse

Thoughts / Reflections

I am thankful for

Prayer Requests

Today's Date

Daily Verse

Thoughts / Reflections

I am thankful for

Prayer Requests

Today's Date

Daily Verse

Thoughts / Reflections

I am thankful for

Prayer Requests

Today's Date

Daily Verse

Thoughts / Reflections

I am thankful for

Prayer Requests

Today's Date

Daily Verse

Thoughts / Reflections

I am thankful for

Prayer Requests

1 John 1 v 9

" If we confess our sins,
he is faithful and just
to forgive us our sins
and to cleanse us
from all unrighteousness."

Today's Date

Daily Verse

Thoughts / Reflections

I am thankful for

Prayer Requests

Today's Date

Daily Verse

Thoughts / Reflections

I am thankful for

Prayer Requests

Today's Date

Daily Verse

Thoughts / Reflections

I am thankful for

Prayer Requests

Today's Date

Daily Verse

Thoughts / Reflections

I am thankful for

Prayer Requests

Today's Date

Daily Verse

Thoughts / Reflections

I am thankful for

Prayer Requests

Today's Date

Daily Verse

Thoughts / Reflections

I am thankful for

Prayer Requests

Today's Date

Daily Verse

Thoughts / Reflections

I am thankful for

Prayer Requests

Today's Date

Daily Verse

Thoughts / Reflections

I am thankful for

Prayer Requests

Today's Date

Daily Verse

Thoughts / Reflections

I am thankful for

Prayer Requests

Lamentations 3 v 22-23

" The steadfast love
of the Lord never ceases;
his mercies never
come to an end;

They are new
every morning;
great is your faithfulness."

Today's Date

Daily Verse

Thoughts / Reflections

I am thankful for

Prayer Requests

Today's Date

Daily Verse

Thoughts / Reflections

I am thankful for

Prayer Requests

Today's Date

Daily Verse

Thoughts / Reflections

I am thankful for

Prayer Requests

Today's Date

Daily Verse

Thoughts / Reflections

I am thankful for

Prayer Requests

Today's Date

Daily Verse

Thoughts / Reflections

I am thankful for

Prayer Requests

| Today's Date | |

| Daily Verse | Thoughts / Reflections |

| I am thankful for | Prayer Requests |

Today's Date

Daily Verse

Thoughts / Reflections

I am thankful for

Prayer Requests

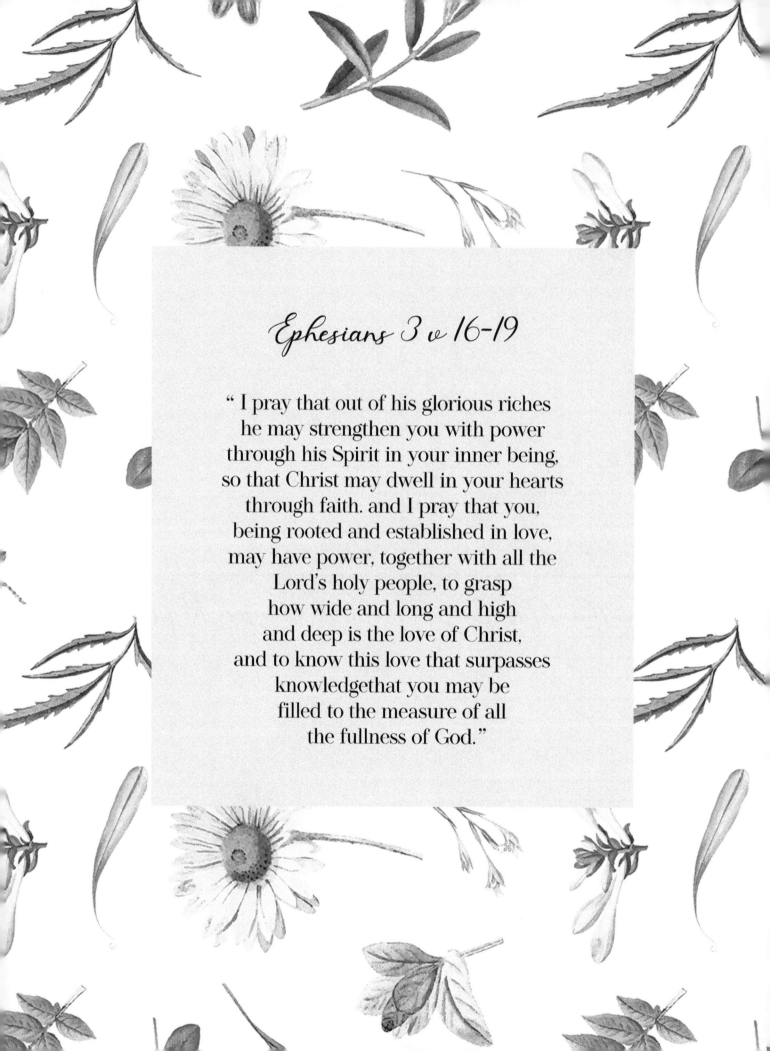

Ephesians 3 v 16-19

" I pray that out of his glorious riches
he may strengthen you with power
through his Spirit in your inner being,
so that Christ may dwell in your hearts
through faith. and I pray that you,
being rooted and established in love,
may have power, together with all the
Lord's holy people, to grasp
how wide and long and high
and deep is the love of Christ,
and to know this love that surpasses
knowledgethat you may be
filled to the measure of all
the fullness of God."